# WORLD'S CUTEST CATS & KITTENS
## in 3-D

Cats are cute and cuddly and make great pets. But they have their wild side, too! Domestic cats are closely related to big cats such as tigers and lions, and they love to pounce and chase like their exotic cousins. Curl up with these lovable creatures and find out more about our feline friends.

# CONTENTS

# FURRY FRIENDS

Millions of people around the world keep cats as pets. Cats can be loyal and loving, and they are beautiful creatures to look at. They were first welcomed into human homes thousands of years ago when people saw how useful they were for getting rid of pesky rats and mice that ate their food.

### LEAVING HOME
Most kittens leave their mothers to live in a new home when they are between eight and 12 weeks old.

### MAKING FRIENDS
If you would like more than one cat, it is a good idea to get brothers and sisters. Unrelated cats may get along fine, but cats can be friendly or grumpy, just like people!

The most popular names for pet cats include Tigger, Shadow, Molly, Misty, and Kitty.

**WILD THINGS**
Pet cats are descended from wild cats. This one has a thick double coat to keep it warm and dry in harsh weather.

## HERE TO STAY
Think carefully before you get a cat as a pet. Cats need your love and care every day, and can live for more than 20 years. Your pet kitty may still need you even when you're grown up and ready to leave home!

**DID YOU KNOW?**
The world's oldest pet cat lived in Texas and lived to be 38 years old!

# ON THE CATWALK

Cats come in different colours and sizes, but they all look remarkably similar. Take a look at the biggest and the smallest you see, and you will notice that they aren't really so different. They're nothing like dog breeds, in which the largest can be 300 times heavier than the tiny ones! Some cat breeds are almost hairless, but most fall into two groups: longhair and shorthair.

## SOFT BUT SMOOTH
Sphynx cats don't have a furry coat like other cats. They do have a fine covering of soft hair but look almost bald. Their skin has markings that show the pattern their fur would have – if they had any! They make great pets, as they are clever, lively, and love cuddles with their owners.

## KEEPING CLEAN
Cats wash themselves by licking their fur. Their tongue has tiny spikes on; it will feel rough if a cat licks you. This allows their tongue to act like a hairbrush to keep their fur clean.

## GREY OR BLUE?

Cat breeders sometimes call the fur colour by different names. This Korat cat has grey fur, but is described as blue by breeders. Korats originally come from Thailand, where they are given as good luck presents, especially at weddings.

## CAT CARE

Long-haired cats need regular brushing by their owners. Start when they are young using a soft cat brush so they can get used to being groomed. The Norwegian forest cat shown here has a shorter woolly layer underneath its long fur to keep it warm in cold weather.

## DID YOU KNOW?

When a cat grooms itself, it will often swallow loose fur. This gathers in its insides and has to be coughed up as a hairball!

**DAILY TASK**
Cat owners who want a long-haired breed often choose Persian cats. They need more care than short-haired cats as their fur easily becomes tangled and knotted. They should be brushed every day if possible.

## DID YOU KNOW?

Some Persian cats have a very flat face. This can cause problems with their eyes and their breathing.

# TOP CAT

Many pet owners choose their cat because of its looks. They might like its colouring, its face shape, its startling eyes, or its silky fur. Different breeds mix together to make new cats with special characteristics. Some of them are pedigrees, carefully chosen for their looks. Others happen purely by accident, and they are often affectionately known as moggies.

### LOYAL FRIEND
A Burmese cat, like the one here, has beautifully smooth, short, shiny fur, and can be many shades of brown. They become very attached to their owners and will follow a person around like a dog, even playing fetch and tag. It isn't a good idea to own a Burmese if it will be left on its own all day.

### OUTDOOR PLAY
Cats have a reputation for disliking water, but the Turkish Van breed seems to love it! Its fur is water-resistant and always white, except on its head and tail. These cats also love climbing, playing, and hunting, and they will often return home with a dirty white coat.

### LITTLE LEGS
Munchkin cats come in all shades and patterns, with long hair or short, but they have one noticeable feature: their legs are extremely short. They are fast and fun-loving, but they can't jump high onto the furniture in one leap!

**CATS THAT CRY**
Siamese cats have bright blue eyes and large ears. The kittens start life with pure white fur, but they develop dark ears, nose, tail, and paws as they grow older. They are noisier than many breeds, and they can make a cry that sounds like a human baby!

**DID YOU KNOW?**
The hairless Peterbald breed of cat has webbed feet, and it can use its paws to hold items and open door handles!

**CAT CHARACTERS**
Some cats flatten their ears to show you what mood they are in, but this Scottish Fold's ears are always like that! The kittens have straight ears, but as they grow up the ears begin to fold over and lie flat on the head.

The first Scottish Fold cat was found in 1961 in Scotland. Since then, it has become a popular but rare breed. These cats make extremely loving pets that enjoy being part of a family. Although the ears are flattened, they still move when they hear a noise, and prick up at any interesting sounds.

# CUTE AS A KITTEN

Most baby animals are as cute as a button, and kittens are no exception! Newborns are tiny and helpless. They can't even see or hear at first, and they need their mothers to protect them. If a mother feels her kittens are in danger, she will pick each one up in her mouth and carry it to a safe place.

### LEARNING ABOUT LIFE
Kittens love to run, play, and explore. This is how they learn about the world around them. When you see them wrestling, pouncing, and chasing moving objects, they are getting ready for their grownup life when they hunt for food – even though, as pets, that will be put in a bowl for them every day!

## DID YOU KNOW?

A group of kittens is called a litter or sometimes a kindle. A group of adult cats may be called a clowder, a clutter, or a glaring!

## HIDE AND SEEK
Young kittens are naturally nosy, but they might hide in dark places and get trapped. Make sure you always know where your kitten has gone!

## BROTHERS AND SISTERS
A mother will have more than one kitten at a time. It is normal for her to give birth to between four and six babies, sometimes more.

## EARLY DAYS
A kitten is born with its eyes closed, and they slowly open after a week or so. They will be blue at first, but that doesn't mean the adult cat will have blue eyes. They will gradually change as the kitten gets older. This happens with human babies, too!

In 1995, a kitten with green fur was born in Denmark! Was it a strange new breed? Experts decided it wasn't. The cause: the water where it lived was polluted with copper, a metal that can turn things green.

# SUPER SENSES

Pet cats are related to wild animals like tigers and leopards. They are designed to eat meat, and their bodies have all sorts of superpowers to make them into fantastic hunters. They can hear, smell, and see much better than you can, even at night!

## NIGHT HUNTING

A cat uses all of its senses to find its way at night and to hunt for food. Its nose is much more sensitive than a person's nose, and a cat can smell things a human can't smell at all.

## THE CAT'S WHISKERS

Cats use their whiskers to feel their way in the dark. These long, wiry hairs sense objects and air movements, so they know what is close by. The whiskers also tell your cat about any food that is too close to its mouth for it to see.

## DID YOU KNOW?

A cat uses its tail to give it extra balance. As its body leans in one direction, its tail moves the opposite way to even things up. Its tail also swirls around like a propeller if the cat jumps or falls to help move its body into a safe landing position.

## CAT'S EYES

Cats can't see in total darkness, but they can see in very poor light. They have an extra layer in their eyes that reflects light and helps them see better. That is what makes their eyes glow if they look at your car headlights. In bright sunlight, your cat's dark pupils will narrow to thin slits.

## I CAN HEAR YOU!

A cat's ears can pick up tiny noises. It can hear high-pitched squeaks and the smallest shuffling noises made by a mouse in the plants nearby!

## CAREFUL CLIMBERS

Remember that great sense of balance we just talked about? Watch your pet as it confidently picks its way along a tiny ledge or thin fence. Its eyes and ears are tuned in to keep it safely upright, and its body shape allows it to place its feet on the narrowest path without wobbling.

## DID YOU KNOW?

A cat doesn't only swish its tail from side to side when it is balancing. It will flick its tail to show that it can't decide what to do, as if its mind – like its tail – is going back and forth.

# ON THE PROWL

Cats are born to hunt. Even if they have a loving owner who provides it healthy meals each day, the cat's natural instincts tell it to go out and look for something to eat. When the cat has to hunt near human homes, that food is usually a bird, a mouse, a rat, or a frog. If your cat really loves you, it will bring home its catch as a present for you!

## DID YOU KNOW?

Don't give your cat too many treats. They are not meant to fill up on 'people food' such as tuna and cheese. Special cat food should make up nearly all of their diet.

## STAY ALERT
Cats are very sensitive to what is around them. They are always on the lookout for something to chase – or that might chase them!

## LYING LOW

A cat stalks its prey. When it catches sight of something moving, it hunkers down close to the ground so it can't be seen easily. It will probably twitch its tail, and then lift one front paw, ready to move.

## THE THRILL OF THE CHASE

Cats are fascinated by moving things. They will chase insects and pin them down to see if they are tasty treats. You can see this when they play with you; that's why they chase a toy on a piece of string.

## PREPARING TO JUMP

While its prey remains unaware that it is being watched, the cat slowly and silently creeps forward. It waits until it is really close before it pounces at top speed.

## NATURAL INSTINCTS

Even if your cat is well-fed, it will still have the urge to hunt. Some cats walk straight out of the kitchen, their tummy full, and chase a bird.

# DID YOU KNOW?

Cows' milk can be very bad for your cat. Kittens get all the goodness they need from their mother, but as they grow up they become unable to digest milk. Give your cat water instead, especially if you feed it dry food.

# PLAY TIME

Healthy cats love to play. If you're lucky, your pet cat will let you play with it. You can have great fun dragging a small soft toy across the floor on a piece of string. It can be fun to just sit and watch your pet amuse itself, too!

## RECONNAISSANCE MISSION

Your cat will probably poke its nose into everything. This is a natural instinct to explore its territory and find safe places, dangerous places, hiding places…and also because cats hate to be shut into just one space. They will often climb inside boxes, bags, and baskets to check them out!

## LEARNING THROUGH PLAY

Playing is good practice for hunting. Cats often clasp tightly onto a toy and then kick at it with their back legs. Jumping, climbing, pouncing, and running are all practice, too.

## DON'T TOUCH!

Cats think everything in their home is theirs to play with. It is hard to teach a cat not to touch things. Sometimes it is just easier to move anything that can get damaged if your cat takes a swipe at it!

## DID YOU KNOW?

Kittens will play with almost anything that moves, from a blade of grass to a rolled-up piece of paper. They love to pounce on their mother's tail – or your jiggling feet!

# DID YOU KNOW?

Many cats are attracted to the smell of a plant called catnip. Some cat toys use catnip to entice your pet to play.

## SHARP AS KNIVES

A cat's claws are one of its most important hunting tools. They keep them sharp by scratching against tough surfaces such as wood. Your cat can pull in its claws to protect them when it walks across hard ground, or to stop them getting stuck in your carpet!

# THE GREAT OUT DOORS

Some cat owners keep their pets indoors at all times, to protect them from traffic and other dangers. If your home is away from the busiest roads, you may decide to let your cat wander outside so it can run, climb, and hunt as nature intended.

## KEEPING GUARD
Cats are very territorial. They have their own places for hunting and exploring. They will mark the area with their scent and fight off any other cats that try to intrude.

## A PLACE IN THE SUN
You will often find a cat having a snooze in a warm, su spot. This helps them to save energy. They will only do they feel safe, so it is more common indoors.

## UP AND DOWN

A cat's sharp claws are a huge help for climbing trees. Their curved shape makes it difficult to climb down again, though, so most cats end up scrabbling down in reverse. This is one of the few times a cat does not look graceful and elegant!

### DID YOU KNOW?

Many breeds of cat are excellent jumpers. Some can leap five times their own height in a single bound!

## HOME TIME
Outdoor cats can explore for miles, so don't be worried if your pet disappears for a while. If it doesn't come back at night, it may have got trapped so you should start to search for it. Nosy cats often end up locked in someone else's shed or garage.

## DID YOU KNOW?

Several plants are harmful to cats if they chew them. Be sure your cat can't nibble on lilies, tulips, daffodils, or tomato plants. Ask your vet to tell you about any other plants that may be dangerous for your pet.

# CAT NAPS

## SNOOZING SPOTS
Give your pet some options for its sleeping place. Cats like to choose between a cosy bed on the floor and one higher up. Or it may just find its own bed somewhere it feels safe!

## HAPPY TOGETHER
Not all cats and dogs fight! They can become close friends if they are raised together.

## RECHARGING
A cat uses its energy in short bursts for hunting. Then it will have a nap afterward to recharge.

You might have noticed your cat sleeps a lot – an awful lot, in fact! Most cats will snooze off and on all day long, for around 15 hours in total. That's twice as much as you! Older cats may sleep even longer.

## DID YOU KNOW?

Cats feel vulnerable if their tummy is exposed. So a cat that sleeps on its back feels safe and secure.

## WARNING SIGNS
In the wild, cats need to be strong to survive. They cover up any signs of weakness, such as feeling ill or injured. Keep a close eye on your cat if it hides all the time, doesn't eat much, or makes its toilet mess all over the house.

## DID YOU KNOW?

If your cat rolls over to show you its belly, it means that it trusts you. Scratch its head instead of tickling its tummy.

# WILD THINGS

All pet cats are related to wild cats such as this bobcat. They still have many things in common with leopards and lio They hunt in the same way and have t same body shape. Even your tabby's markings are camouflage to help it remain undetected when lurkir in long grass.

## A TASTY TREAT
A cat may lick its lips if it spies a bird outside. It does it while it watches and waits – even if a window is between them!

## MAKING ITS MARK
Scratching will keep a cat's claws sharp and also leaves marks to show other animals that they are on the cat's territory.

## SUPER CLEAN
Cats hate to be dirty. They lick themselves to keep their fur clean and smooth. It also helps them to cool down. Cats groom each other to show friendship and trust.

## DID YOU KNOW?
Small cats make a distinctive purring noise, but they cannot roar like large cats. Tigers, leopards, and jaguars can all roar, but lions have the loudest roar of them all!

**ON THE MOVE**
A mother cat can carry her kittens in her mouth in the same way that a lioness carries her cubs. She grabs the loose skin at the back of the neck and lifts the baby off the ground. The mother bites gently so she doesn't hurt her baby.

## DID YOU KNOW?

The kitten knows instinctively to tuck up its legs and tail and stay still instead of wriggling while it's being carried by its mother. This makes it easier for its mother to move it around.

# CAT CALLS

People tell each other how they feel with their voices, by talking or shouting or laughing. They also move their faces into smiles, scowls, and frowns to communicate. Cats cannot do these things, but they do have other ways of showing how they are feeling.

## DID YOU KNOW?

A happy cat will close its eyes partway even if it is not sleepy. It shows that it is relaxed and not worried about attackers creeping up on it.

## DIFFERENT SOUNDS

A cat is likely to purr, hiss, or spit if it is talking to another animal. Altogether, cats can make around 100 sounds; that's 10 times more than a dog can make.

## LARGER THAN LIFE
A scared cat will try to make itself look bigger to frighten off its enemy. The hairs on its back and tail stand on end, and it arches its back and bares its teeth.

## TALKING TO YOU
Cats make many noises that mean many things. They most often make their meowing sound to get the attention of humans!

## ESKIMO KISS
Rubbing together, especially with their noses, is a common way for cats to say hello.

## DID YOU KNOW?

Kittens and their mothers often purr to show that they feel safe and are happy. A kitten will make more impatient mewing noises to get its mother's attention.

## BODY LANGUAGE
A cat can tell you a lot with its body, not just its mouth. Its ears twitch if it is nervous and lie flat on its head if it is ready to attack. Its tail will move in many different ways to show fear, happiness, excitement, or anger.

# COOL CATS

Cats can be found on every continent, although they were only introduced to Australia, Antarctica, and the Americas by people who wanted them to keep down the numbers of rodents. This isn't always successful; cats killed so many precious seabirds in the Antarctic that the cats themselves had to be removed. Generally, though, cats are loved by humans and kept as pampered pets in many countries.

## SACRED CREATURES

Cats were so important in ancient Egypt that a person could be sentenced to death for killing one. If the pet cat died, the whole family went into mourning, which included shaving off their eyebrows!

## ENORMOUS!

The biggest breed of cat is the Maine Coon. It is huge! It can weigh as much as a 2-year-old child, and its beautiful bushy tail can be more than a foot long.

## TAIL-LESS!

Some cats have no tail! The Manx cat breed can have a short stump or no tail at all, and the Japanese bobtail has a small tuft that is more like the tail of a rabbit.

## FEELING LUCKY?

In the UK, seeing a black cat is meant to bring good luck, but in many other countries, black cats equal bad luck. All-white cats are considered lucky in Asian countries.